FIGHTER PILOT

BY NICK GORDON

BELLWETHER MEDIA · MINNEAPOLIS, MN

Are you ready to take it to the extreme?
Torque books thrust you into the action-packed world
of sports, vehicles, mystery, and adventure. These books
may include dirt, smoke, fire, and dangerous stunts.
WARNING: read at your own risk.

Library of Congress Cataloging-in-Publication Data

Gordon, Nick.
 Fighter pilot / by Nick Gordon.
    p. cm. -- (Torque: dangerous jobs)
 Includes bibliographical references and index.
 Summary: "Engaging images accompany information about fighter pilots. The combination of high-interest
subject matter and light text is intended for students in grades 3 through 7"--Provided by publisher.
 ISBN 978-1-60014-894-1 (hbk. : alk. paper)
 1. Fighter pilots--Juvenile literature. I. Title.
 UG631.G67 2013
 358.4'31--dc23
                                            2012041221

This edition first published in 2013 by Bellwether Media, Inc.

Printed in the United States of America, North Mankato, MN.

TABLE OF CONTENTS

CHAPTER 1

SHOT DOWN

An F-22 Raptor's jet engines roar as a fighter pilot makes a hard dive. Far below, the enemy fires **antiaircraft weapons**. Suddenly, explosions light up the sky. A **missile** slams into one of the Raptor's wings. The plane is going to crash!

The pilot must **eject**. He pulls a lever. The **cockpit** opens and his seat flies into the air. The pilot's **parachute** opens and he floats safely to the ground. He uses his radio to call for help.

Dogfight

Pilots use the term *dogfight* to describe combat between two or more fighter planes at close range. Today, dogfights are rare. Most combat takes place at a distance.

CHAPTER 2

FIGHTER PILOTS

RESCUE

1. PUSH BUTTON TO OPEN DOOR
2. PULL RING OUT 6 FEET TO
JETTISON CANOPY

Fighter pilots are among the most skilled pilots in the world. They fly heavily armed fighter jets for military forces. One of their jobs is to attack enemy targets in the air and on the ground. Their **mission** is to protect troops.

Only the Best

Fighter pilots must be intelligent. They must also have excellent vision and hand-eye coordination.

It takes years of training to become a fighter pilot. Pilots must practice flying in all kinds of weather. They learn how to fire missiles, guns, and other weapons. They are trained to read a plane's **instruments**. Fighter pilots in the U.S. Navy must be able to take off from and land on **aircraft carriers**.

aircraft carrier

Real-Time Training

Fighter pilots train for real-life situations in flight simulators. These devices have the same controls and instruments found in fighter jets.

Safety gear protects fighter pilots. **G-suits** help them deal with extreme **g-forces**. They squeeze the body to keep blood flowing to the brain. Pilots also wear flight helmets and masks. The masks provide oxygen for pilots to breathe.

Fighter pilots have special gear for when they eject. Parachutes carry them safely to the ground. Pilots have flotation devices in case they land in water. The vests they wear hold a radio, **flares**, and other survival items.

CHAPTER 3

DANGER!

Fighter pilots often have to push their jets to the limit. They face strong g-forces when they climb higher or turn. These forces put a lot of stress on their bodies. They can cause pilots to **black out**. This is a disaster while in the air!

High-G

G-forces are measured in g's. One g is the normal force of gravity. Fighter pilots must endure up to 9 g's. That means they weigh nine times more than they do when on the ground!

Pilots face other dangers. A fighter jet can **malfunction**. Damage to engines or landing gear can cause crashes. Pilots are at the greatest risk while on missions. Enemies on the ground and in the air may try to shoot them down.

Fighter pilots understand the dangers of the job. They accept the risk. They love flying the world's most advanced fighter jets. Pilots do all they can to complete their missions and return home safely.

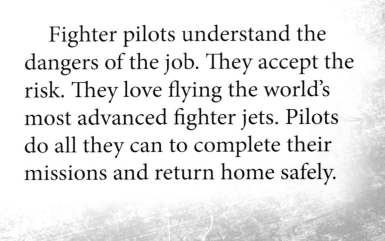

Tragedy on the Job

In 2010, a U.S. Air Force pilot was flying a training mission in an F-22. The aircraft malfunctioned and cut off his oxygen supply. The pilot blacked out before he could save himself. He died when the F-22 crashed to the ground.

Glossary

aircraft carriers—large ships that aircraft can take off from and land on

antiaircraft weapons—weapons that are designed to shoot down airplanes and helicopters

black out—to have blurred vision and then pass out

cockpit—the area inside an aircraft where the pilot sits

eject—to be launched out of an aircraft before a crash

flares—devices that burn very brightly; pilots use flares after ejecting so rescuers can find them.

g-forces—the pressures that high speeds and quick turns place on a pilot

g-suits—special suits that help keep blood flowing to pilots' brains during high-g maneuvers

instruments—the gauges on an aircraft that give information such as speed and altitude

malfunction—to stop working properly

missile—an explosive that is guided to its target

mission—a military task

parachute—a cloth canopy that fills with air and slows the fall of a person or object

To Learn More

AT THE LIBRARY

Anderson, Jameson. *Fighter Pilot*. Chicago, Ill.: Raintree, 2007.

Loveless, Antony. *Fighter Pilots*. New York, N.Y.: Crabtree Pub. Co., 2010.

Reeves, Diane Lindsey. *Scary Jobs*. New York, N.Y.: Ferguson, 2009.

ON THE WEB

Learning more about fighter pilots is as easy as 1, 2, 3.

1. Go to www.factsurfer.com.

2. Enter "fighter pilots" into the search box.

3. Click the "Surf" button and you will see a list of related Web sites.

With factsurfer.com, finding more information is just a click away.

Index